AF228526

INSIDE MLS

NASHVILLE SC

BY ANTHONY K. HEWSON

SportsZone
An Imprint of Abdo Publishing
abdobooks.com

abdobooks.com

Published by Abdo Publishing, a division of ABDO, PO Box 398166, Minneapolis, Minnesota 55439. Copyright © 2022 by Abdo Consulting Group, Inc. International copyrights reserved in all countries. No part of this book may be reproduced in any form without written permission from the publisher. SportsZone™ is a trademark and logo of Abdo Publishing.

Printed in the United States of America, North Mankato, Minnesota
052021
092021

Cover Photo: Jacob Kupferman/Cal Sport Media/Zuma Wire/AP Images
Interior Photos: Jacob Kupferman/Cal Sport Media/Zuma Wire/AP Images, 5, 9, 13; Kevin Langley/Cal Sport Media/Zuma Wire/AP Images, 7, 11, 37; Bill Waugh/AP Images, 15; Andy Mead/ISI Photos/Getty Images Sport/Getty Images, 16; Matthew Ashton/AMA/Getty Images Sport/Getty Images, 18; Kevin Schultz/Cal Sport Media/Zuma Wire/AP Images, 20; Mark Zaleski/AP Images, 22–23; Rich Graessle/Icon Sportswire/AP Images, 25; Cliff Welch/Icon Sportswire/AP Images, 26; Rich von Biberstein/Icon Sportswire/AP Images, 28; Matthew Maxey/Icon Sportswire/AP Images, 30–31; Brynn Anderson/AP Images, 33; Shelley Mays/The Tennessean/USA Today Network/Sipa USA/Alamy, 35; Matt Cullom/MediaPunch/Ipx/AP Images, 38; Diego Diaz/Icon Sportswire/AP Images, 40; Omar Vega/Getty Images Sport/Getty Images, 43

Editor: Patrick Donnelly
Series Designer: Dan Peluso

Library of Congress Control Number: 2020948283

Publisher's Cataloging-in-Publication Data

Names: Hewson, Anthony K., author.
Title: Nashville SC / by Anthony K. Hewson
Description: Minneapolis, Minnesota : Abdo Publishing, 2022 | Series: Inside MLS |
    Includes online resources and index.
Identifiers: ISBN 9781532194771 (lib. bdg.) | ISBN 9781098214432 (ebook)
Subjects: LCSH: Soccer teams--Juvenile literature. | Professional sports franchises--
    Juvenile literature. | Sports Teams--Juvenile literature.
Classification: DDC 796.334--dc23

TABLE OF CONTENTS

CHAPTER 1

NASHVILLE LEAPS
TO MLS

Walker Zimmerman was in unfamiliar territory. As a center back, he wasn't used to scoring goals. But there he was in the penalty area, awaiting his chance to change the game.

And it wasn't just any game. It was the first Major League Soccer (MLS) game for Nashville Soccer Club (SC). The new team was hosting Atlanta United on February 29, 2020.

The free kick came in from teammate Hany Mukhtar. Zimmerman moved toward the ball, meeting it with his head. At first it looked like he'd misplayed the ball. Instead of darting toward goal, the ball hit down toward the ground.

But Zimmerman knew what he was doing. He played the ball to himself. He was in perfect position to poke it past

Hany Mukhtar celebrates the first MLS goal in Nashville SC history.

Atlanta goalkeeper Brad Guzan. When it crossed the goal line, the crowd of 59,069 roared.

Two years earlier, a crowd that size—the largest ever to see a soccer game in Tennessee—would have been unthinkable. The team's origins were in a grassroots, supporter-led team. Eventually moving up to the second division, the newly named Nashville SC played its first friendly February 10, 2018, also against Atlanta United. By then Nashville was already ticketed for MLS, a whirlwind process that went from an idea to a real MLS team on the field in less than four years.

NASHVILLE'S PARTY

Though Nashville fans didn't have to wait long for a team, excitement had quickly built up in the Music City. Nashville's first MLS game turned into a huge party. Fans started gathering near Nissan Stadium early in the day, grilling food and kicking around soccer balls.

It's no surprise that in a city known for making music, musicians served as the opening act. With fans still making their way to their seats, local band Judah and the Lion played a pregame concert. On the setlist was the song they wrote with the team to serve as the official club anthem, "Never Give Up on You."

Soccer fans in Nashville found different ways to get fired up for the club's first MLS match.

"Hey brother, hey sister, I'll never give up on you," were the opening lyrics.

Fans joined in singing the anthem. Then they joined in on another anthem, "The Star-Spangled Banner." The crowd's participation grew as the song went on, with some fans holding up their team scarves. The players took notice.

"Amazing atmosphere from them," Zimmerman said. "It was fun watching the anthem as we were sitting in a tunnel, and just watching the crowd singing that and getting involved, and that's only going to grow."

Finally, guitarist Lzzy Hale performed an "opening riff" from among the Backline, Nashville's supporters' section. The improvised guitar solo was to become a regular part of Nashville match day. Different musicians would be invited each home game to get the crowd excited with some guitar licks.

THE KICKOFF

With the pregame festivities done, it was time for the main event. Atlanta United was a great test for Nashville. They were one of the league's best teams. They also were a model for an expansion team. Atlanta qualified for the playoffs in its first season in 2017 and won the MLS Cup the next year.

Atlanta's potent scoring attack quieted the 60,000 fans just nine minutes into the game. Midfielder Ezequiel Barco found himself with space in the middle of the field. He shook free of a defender and rifled a shot past Nashville keeper Joe Willis. A small gathering of United fans who made the trip from Georgia roared in a corner of the stadium.

Randall Leal looks for room to maneuver against Atlanta United.

But the new club did not go away. Nashville settled down and pushed for a tying goal. Randall Leal and Dom Badji each had attempts. That hard work paid off with Zimmerman's breakthrough goal in the 28th minute. That got the stadium rocking once again. Zimmerman raised his arms to tell the crowd to keep the noise coming.

Zimmerman was Nashville's key player. He was a true MLS star, a US national team regular in the prime of his career. One year earlier he had made his first All-Star Game while playing with Los Angeles Football Club (LAFC). Nashville built its roster around possession and defense. Zimmerman anchored the defense while Mukhtar and MLS veteran Dax McCarty locked down midfield.

Nashville was able to mostly contain Atlanta's elite scorers. But its own forwards also struggled to convert chances. They couldn't rely on defenders like Zimmerman to do all the scoring.

IN A FIGHT

The fans got quiet again in the 37th minute. On an Atlanta corner kick, Nashville failed to clear the ball. An assistant referee added some confusion by raising the offside flag, only to put it back down as play continued. The ball bounced

Teammates mob Walker Zimmerman, *third from right*, after he got Nashville SC on the board.

around the penalty area before landing at the feet of Atlanta's Emerson Hyndman. He buried a shot and United regained the lead.

The score was 2–1 at halftime. Nashville came out in the second half and worked to get an equalizer. The crowd was right behind them, chanting "N-S-C!" throughout the half.

Nashville fired 15 shots in the game. Atlanta managed just six. But United led in goals, the only stat that mattered. Nashville tried everything, including subbing off Badji for speedy forward Abu Danladi.

Leal had one of the best chances of the game in the 78th minute. First he shook his defender in the box. Then Leal took a shot with his left foot that beat the keeper. But it didn't beat the post, and the ball deflected out of play.

Former Nashville minor leaguer Daniel Ríos, a top scorer for that version of the club, came on for Leal late in the game. Still, it wasn't enough to get the tying goal. Nashville fell in its first game, 2–1. But with a big, enthusiastic crowd and impressive periods of play, Nashville showed MLS it was ready.

Nashville goalkeeper Joe Willis makes a save against Atlanta United.

CHAPTER 2

MUSIC CITY
SOCCER

The Nashville Metros appeared to be doing fine for a minor league club. Then, seemingly overnight, they were gone. Founded in 1989, Nashville's first pro soccer team was one of the oldest continuously operating soccer clubs in the United States when it folded in 2012.

But there was no big goodbye for the Metros. Fans simply learned their team was gone when the Premier Development League (PDL) unveiled its 2013 schedule and the Metros weren't on it. Though they had garnered a small fanbase, the Metros likely weren't destined for MLS. At the time of their demise, the PDL was in the fourth tier of American soccer.

Despite losing its only team, Nashville had plenty of soccer fans. The Nashville area had one of the fastest-growing

Nashville has been an enthusiastic host for the US men's and women's national teams.

Belmont is one of three Division I college soccer programs in Nashville.

populations in the United States. Many of the people moving to Nashville were immigrants who brought with them a passion for soccer from their home nations, where soccer was the most popular sport.

Tennessee once had some of the lowest youth soccer participation numbers in the Southeast. But those numbers surged in the 2000s. Since 2003, more than 70 high schools had added boys' soccer, girls' soccer, or both. That increased participation by 65 percent. Nashville had also hosted a handful of US men's and women's national team games over the years. And the city also was home to three Division I college soccer programs in Vanderbilt, Belmont, and Lipscomb.

A FAN AND A DREAM

Nashville's MLS dreams dated back to 1998. That was when the league expanded for the first time, ultimately choosing Miami and Chicago to host new clubs. Nashville wanted to be in the mix. At the time, the Metros were playing just one level below MLS. And they had 1,000 season-ticket holders, which was a large number for a minor league team.

All the while, Nashville was also becoming a major league city. In 1998 the Houston Oilers of the National Football League (NFL) completed their move to Nashville, where they became the Tennessee Titans. And the National Hockey League's Nashville Predators began their inaugural season that fall.

But Nashville was not granted an MLS team. Instead, the Metros continued their minor league existence until 2012. Then, suddenly, a city with an emerging number of soccer fans had no team at all.

Nissan Stadium, the massive home of the NFL's Tennessee Titans, was the most logical site to host a new MLS team.

That didn't sit right with Chris Jones. Jones had no soccer background. He was just a fan. He followed English soccer and also saw the passionate atmosphere that MLS teams such as the Seattle Sounders had created. Jones wanted the same for Nashville.

With no local team to follow, Jones and a friend set out to form their own. They knew that some teams in Europe were owned by fans, and they decided to follow that model. Jones worked to build the club from scratch. While holding a full-time job in banking, he worked on club business on his lunch break, at night, and whenever else he could find the time. He sold shares in the club for $40. Enough people bought into his vision that Nashville FC was playing games by 2014.

The club started out small. It played in the National Premier Soccer League (NPSL), a semipro league three divisions below MLS. But Jones had big dreams for the club. He wanted Nashville playing in the United Soccer League (USL), just one level below MLS, by 2019.

NEW OWNERS, SAME GOAL

The USL came calling earlier than expected. In 2016 Nashville was indeed awarded a bid for a USL team. But it didn't go to Jones and Nashville FC. It was awarded to another ownership group. However, that group approached Nashville FC with an idea. It wanted to buy the name, logo, and colors and take

Nashville SC's Liam Doyle attempts a penalty shot in a 2018 USL playoff match against FC Cincinnati.

the club to the USL. The Nashville FC members voted and overwhelmingly approved the sale. They retained 1 percent of the new club.

In a downtown celebration, the USL announced that
Nashville FC would be joining the league for 2018. But plenty
of other changes took place before then. One major change
was that the new owners swapped "football" for "soccer,"
and changed the club name to Nashville SC. They also made
changes to the logo. But an even bigger change overshadowed
Nashville SC's USL debut.

In the summer of 2016, a group of Nashville business leaders
began a push to put an MLS team in the Music City. In 2017 one
of them bought a stake in Nashville SC, and both parties united
in their effort to take the club to MLS. The group also added
the Wilf family, who owned the NFL's Minnesota Vikings. The
Wilfs had an MLS bid of their own rejected in Minneapolis.

A DREAM COME TRUE

Nashville put together a strong MLS bid. It had good financial
backing and a plan to build a stadium. In December 2017, the
league scheduled an announcement at the Country Music
Hall of Fame. Nashville was going to MLS.

"Nashville is a rising city with a passionate soccer fan base,"
said MLS commissioner Don Garber. "For us, that makes it a
perfect place for MLS expansion."

Fans hugged and celebrated. They had led the way all along. Fans who got together to own a soccer team started the journey to MLS. Now they just had to wait until 2020 for the MLS action to begin.

Fortunately Nashville SC made its USL debut in the spring of 2018. Even though this version of the club was slated to play just two seasons, it helped give fans a preview of what was to come. And the fans liked what they saw. Minor league head coach Gary Smith was retained to coach the team in MLS.

Fans cheer as Nashville SC announces a pick in the MLS expansion draft on November 19, 2019.

Daniel Ríos was one of six players who also made the jump to MLS. Ríos proved to be a goal-scoring phenom, racking up 20 goals in 31 appearances in 2018.

In 2019 the club also confirmed it would be keeping its blue and gold colors in MLS. As for its new name, the fans had their say. They overwhelmingly voted to stay Nashville SC. The club took that history with it to MLS.

CHAPTER 3

THE BLUE
AND GOLD

LAFC was holding a late 1–0 lead over the New England Revolution. Walker Zimmerman was defending as a Revs player ran in the box. For a moment, Zimmerman lost his man. The opponent ran toward the goal, but Zimmerman didn't panic. He ran with him, then slid and swung his right leg in the runner's path to kick the ball away. It was a small moment, but the kind of game-saving tackle elite defenders make.

Players like Zimmerman don't become available every day. It cost Nashville SC big time to get him. The February 2020 trade with LAFC was the biggest for a defender in league history. It cost Nashville at least $950,000. But in

US national team defender Walker Zimmerman was the first big-name player acquired by Nashville SC.

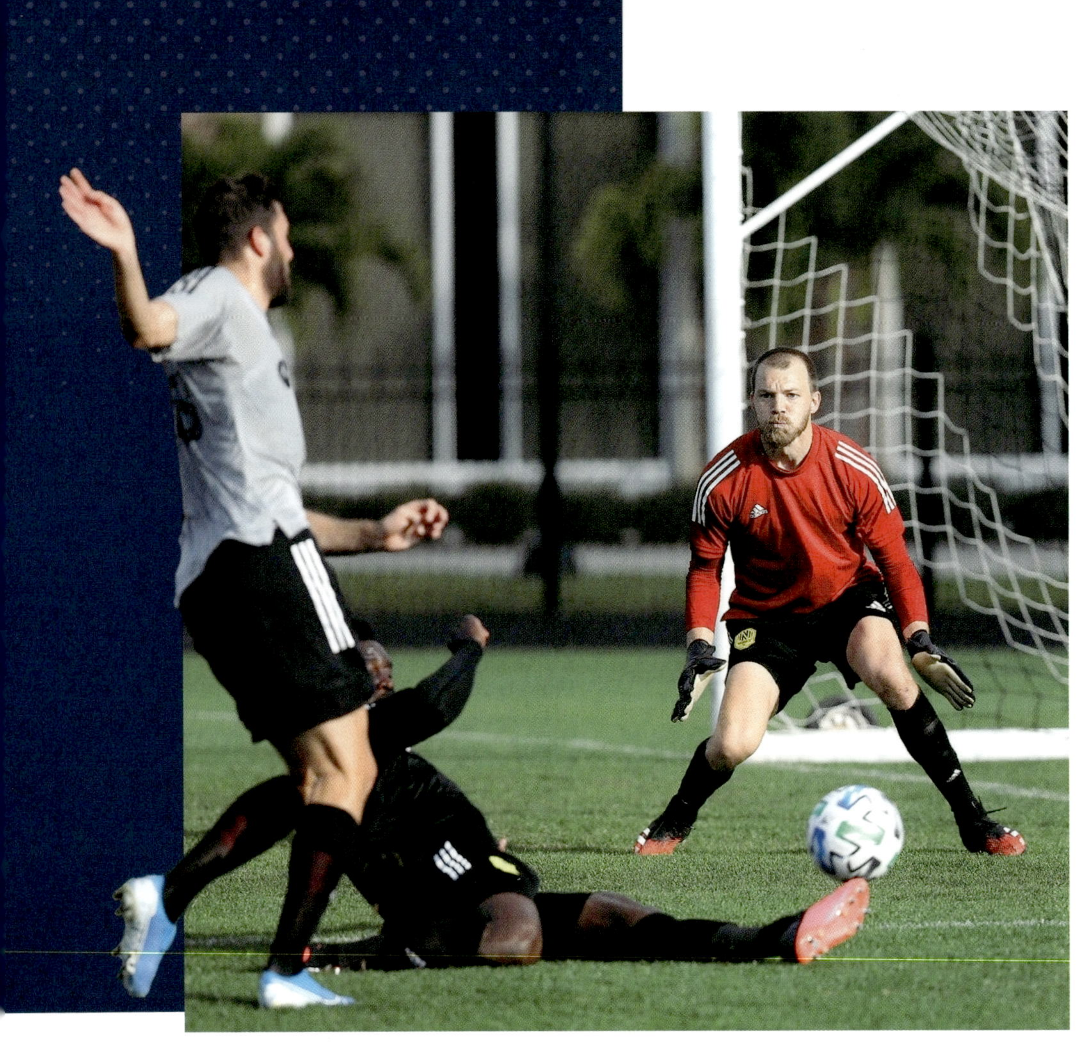

Joe Willis prepares to make a save in a 2020 preseason match against the Chicago Fire.

Zimmerman, the team saw a player around whom they could build their entire team.

At age 26, Zimmerman was coming off his best season and entering his prime. The center back also had a growing role with the US men's national team. Nashville did not spend the kind of money that Atlanta United did when it entered MLS in 2017. But smart signings like Zimmerman showed their intent to compete in MLS right away.

Clearances like the one against New England were a specialty of Zimmerman's. In 2020, he had the second most in MLS. He helped Nashville allow less than a goal per game. It all added up to a dominant season. One year after finishing as runner-up, Zimmerman was named MLS Defender of the Year.

Having a defender like Zimmerman on board was a big boost for goalkeeper Joe Willis. Willis was an MLS veteran whose career began in 2011. After spending most of his career as a backup, Willis got an opportunity to start with Nashville. And he led MLS in shutouts in 2020 with nine.

A DEEP MIDFIELD

With consistent players in goal and on defense, Nashville looked to build a solid midfield. Playing well in those areas would keep the club competitive in a lot of games.

There weren't many players with more MLS experience at midfield than Dax McCarty. He had played in MLS since 2006 for four teams. Nashville acquired McCarty in a trade with the Chicago Fire.

Veteran midfielder Dax McCarty was brought in for his extensive experience.

McCarty brought leadership for the team's younger players and also a lot of effort in midfield. He was known for his two-way play. He was rock-solid on defense but could also lead the offensive attack. An active midfielder, McCarty was often among the top players in touches and pass attempts.

Joining McCarty in the center of midfield was Aníbal Godoy. He arrived in a trade with the San Jose Earthquakes. Godoy made 101 appearances for the Quakes while also being a regular on the Panama national team. McCarty and Godoy ended up leading Nashville in completed passes in 2020.

WAITING IN THE WINGS

One of the ways Nashville tried to be competitive early was looking for young talent. It was a risk not knowing whether these players would turn into stars. But they were less

expensive, and the team could afford to be patient while they developed.

German midfielder Hany Mukhtar became the team's first Designated Player. After starting in his home country, he had bounced around a bit before finding his footing while playing in Denmark. The 24-year-old winger thrived in Nashville, tying for the team lead in goals with four in 2020.

Hany Mukhtar takes a penalty kick against Inter Miami CF in 2020.

The team's second Designated Player was Randall Leal. The winger had played professionally in Belgium and in his native Costa Rica. But he was only 23 and still developing his game. He totaled six goals and six assists in 38 games. Leal also played with the Costa Rica national team.

Nashville grabbed a better-known winger in David Accam. The Ghana national teamer started his professional career in

England, then went to Sweden before moving to MLS. Accam showed a lot of scoring potential. In his first three MLS seasons, all with the Chicago Fire, Accam scored 33 goals. But over the next three years with different teams, he scored just seven goals. Nashville traded for Accam hoping he could rediscover his scoring touch.

Potential was the name of the game for forward Abu Danladi. Nashville was the second expansion team Danladi had played for. In 2017 he was the top draft pick of Minnesota United. Danladi showed flashes of talent in his rookie season, scoring eight goals. He finished second in voting for the MLS Rookie of the Year Award.

But Danladi scored only three goals over the next two seasons. He struggled with injuries. That led to Minnesota leaving him unprotected for the expansion draft. Nashville snapped him up, hoping the speedy 24-year-old striker would recapture his early promise.

Nashville built a roster that was a blend of promising youngsters and experienced veterans. Some players like Zimmerman were a mix of both. Fans hoped it was just the right formula for success.

David Accam, *right*, fights for a ball against Atlanta United's George Bello.

CHAPTER 4

JUST
BEGINNING

The fans started gathering early at Marathon Music Works near downtown Nashville on February 20, 2019. They wanted to get a good spot to see the headline act. But this wasn't one of the venue's many music concerts. It was the birth of Nashville's MLS team.

The team had become official more than a year earlier. But nobody knew exactly what it would look like or what it would be called. Many fans had a say in that process. The club reached out to them to get their opinions.

It turned out that a lot of them wanted the club to look very similar to its predecessor. The minor league Nashville SC team colors were white, blue, and yellow. The new club kept similar colors. But it used new, unique shades that were

A fan waves a flag sporting the Nashville SC logo before the team's first match.

NASHVILLE SOCCER CLUB
SC
SC
MMXIII

officially called electric gold and acoustic blue.

As for the team's name, that would stay the same too. The Nashville SC moniker was going with the club to MLS. However, the players would wear a different badge on their chests. The step up to the first tier of North American soccer called for a new logo. The club designed a unique crest to represent the city. Above the words "Nashville SC" was a big N. The N was made up of parallel lines that also looked like a sound wave, fitting for Music City.

"Since I first got involved in this effort, I have said that I wanted to do something 'In Nashville, for Nashville, with Nashville,'" team owner John Ingram said. "The Nashville SC name and primary gold color, along with the themes of sound and energy in the logo, embody our city and our fans who have been with us from the start."

A member of the Roadies shows his support for Nashville SC.

FANS FOLLOW

Nashville soccer fans enjoyed one more year of Nashville SC in the USL. The club finished second in the Eastern Conference. Forward Daniel Ríos proved to be an electric player, scoring 20 goals. He netted the match-winner in the first round of the playoffs. But in the conference semifinals, the club played its last USL game ever, losing to the Indy Eleven 1–0.

With the club's USL journey complete, it began preparing for MLS play. The team departed for Florida in January to begin its first MLS training camp. In preparation for its big debut, Nashville played friendlies against other league clubs.

It was a good test for a new team. But none of the matches had fans. That had to wait for the regular season. Still that didn't stop some diehards from welcoming the team upon its return to Nashville. Hundreds of supporters were at the airport as the players arrived from Florida to start the season. More than 40,000 tickets had already been sold for the team's home opener the following week.

"Having the fans here to welcome us definitely gives us even more of a home feeling," said Walker Zimmerman. "We're excited for next week."

THE SEASON BEGINS

Fans and players alike were excited for the home opener on February 29. Nearly 60,000 of them roared when Zimmerman scored the team's first goal. Nobody was satisfied with the result, a 2–1 loss to Atlanta United. But Nashville showed it could play with one of the league's best teams.

Parts of Nashville were devastated by a tornado three days after Nashville SC's first game.

Things didn't get any easier the next week. Nashville had to fly across the country to play the Portland Timbers. The Timbers' rabid fans made Portland one of the toughest places to play in MLS. And the minds of Nashville's players were elsewhere as they prepared for the match, thanks to a natural disaster that struck in their own backyard.

Randall Leal reacts to a missed opportunity in Nashville SC's 1–0 loss at Portland.

On March 3, a tornado ripped through the city of Nashville. Twenty-five people were killed, hundreds were injured, and many others lost their homes. Nashville winger David Accam was one of them. He shared images of the damage to his home on social media.

The club had to fly to Portland just days later. The normally intimidating Timbers Army welcomed the visitors with a banner on match day saying "Rose City (loves) Music City." Players from both teams wore patches on their jerseys that said "Never Give Up on You" from the official Nashville anthem. The jerseys were auctioned off after the game to help victims of the tornado.

On the field, Nashville played hard. Much like the match with Atlanta, Nashville had most of the shots and chances. But Portland found the net in the 12th minute. Nashville worked for the rest of the match to get an equalizer, but it failed to do so. The club headed home still looking for its first win.

AN UNUSUAL SEASON

Nashville SC was scheduled to face Toronto FC on March 14. But on March 12, MLS suspended all play in the league. The COVID-19 virus was spreading around the world, including in the United States. Out of concern for health and safety, MLS shut down for months.

The league restarted in July with a tournament. But Nashville had too many players test positive for the virus to take part. The club had to wait until August for its next game. It proved to be worth the wait. David Accam scored in the 86th minute to beat FC Dallas 1–0. Nashville finally had its first victory.

The team lost only five matches the rest of the season. The defense made all the difference. Nashville allowed only 22 goals in 23 games. That helped make up for the team scoring just 24 goals of its own. With an 8–8–7 record, Nashville qualified for the playoffs. It became just the sixth MLS expansion team to make the playoffs in its first season.

Nashville again rode its rock-solid defense to go on a playoff run. First it beat Inter Miami 3–0. Then it played a tight match against Toronto FC that went to extra time 0–0. Daniel Ríos, Nashville's minor league hero, became its MLS hero. His goal in the 108th minute sent Nashville on.

The conference semifinal against Columbus was another 0–0 match. But in extra time, Columbus was able to score two goals. The Crew won 2–0.

David Accam, *left*, celebrates with his teammates after he gave his club a lead against FC Dallas.

It was a heartbreaking finish. But Nashville showed it was not just ready to compete in MLS. It was ready to make a championship run.

TIMELINE

<table>
<tr><th>2014</th><th>2016</th><th>2017</th><th>2017</th><th>2018</th></tr>
<tr><td>Nashville FC, a fan-owned soccer team playing in the National Premier Soccer League, plays its first home game on May 24.</td><td>Under new ownership, the team changes its name to Nashville SC and joins the USL.</td><td>Nashville businessman John Ingram buys a majority share of Nashville SC with the intention to bid for an MLS team.</td><td>On December 20, MLS officially awards an expansion team to Nashville to begin play in 2020.</td><td>Nashville SC plays its first USL home game on March 24 in front of 18,922 fans at Nissan Stadium.</td></tr>
</table>

<table>
<tr><th>2018</th><th>2019</th><th>2020</th><th>2020</th><th>2020</th></tr>
<tr><td>On November 20, Nashville signs its own USL player Daniel Ríos as its first MLS player.</td><td>The club announces it will retain the Nashville SC name in MLS, along with the same colors.</td><td>On February 11, Nashville completes a trade with LAFC for All-Star defender Walker Zimmerman.</td><td>Nashville wins its first MLS game 1–0 over FC Dallas.</td><td>Nashville becomes the sixth MLS team to make the playoffs in its first season, advancing all the way to the conference semis.</td></tr>
</table>

TEAM FACTS

FIRST SEASON

2020

STADIUM

Nissan Stadium (2020–)

KEY PLAYERS

David Accam (2020)
Abu Danladi (2020–)
Randall Leal (2020–)
Dax McCarty (2020–)
Hany Mukhtar (2020–)
Daniel Ríos (2020–)
Walker Zimmerman (2020–)

KEY COACHES

Gary Smith (2020–)

MLS DEFENDER OF THE YEAR

Walker Zimmerman (2020)

USL SEASONS

2 (2018–19)

USL GOALKEEPER OF THE YEAR

Matt Pickens (2019)

USL FIRST TEAM

Matt Pickens (2019)
Daniel Ríos (2019)

GLOSSARY

assists
Passes that lead directly to goals.

center back
A defender who plays in the middle of the field.

corner kick
A free kick from a corner of the field near the opponent's goal.

Designated Player
An MLS player whose salary counts outside the salary cap, allowing teams to sign stars.

expansion team
A new team that is added to an existing league.

free kick
An unguarded kick awarded to a team after an opponent's foul.

friendly
A game that doesn't count in the standings.

offside
An infraction that is called when a player is closer to the goal than the last defender (other than the keeper) when the ball is kicked.

penalty area
The box in front of the goal where a player is granted a penalty kick if he or she is fouled.

subbing off
Removing a player from a game in favor of a player who started the game on the bench.

tackle
An attempt to take the ball away from an opponent.

MORE INFORMATION

BOOKS

Kortemeier, Todd. *Total Soccer*. Minneapolis, MN: Abdo Publishing, 2017.

Marthaler, Jon. *Ultimate Soccer Road Trip*. Minneapolis, MN: Abdo Publishing, 2019.

Marthaler, Jon. *US Men's Professional Soccer*. Minneapolis, MN: Abdo Publishing, 2019.

ONLINE RESOURCES

To learn more about Nashville SC, please visit **abdobooklinks.com** or scan this QR code. These links are routinely monitored and updated to provide the most current information available.

INDEX

ABOUT THE AUTHOR

Anthony K. Hewson has followed American soccer since before the MLS days. Originally from San Diego, he now lives in the Bay Area with his wife and dogs.